This journal belongs to

Introduction

"The way is perfect, like vast space, where nothing is lacking and nothing is in excess. Make the slightest distinction however, and heaven and earth are set infinitely apart."

These words are part of a poem written over 1,400 years ago by an early Zen master known as Sosan. They seem to connect with a core part of our being and convey the duality of life perfectly.

'The way' is existence, life, creation. There is something infinite, profound and perfect about it. It is a feeling beyond words or description that we sense in our hearts at times, like a timeless eternal truth that we have known forever. But overlaying this vast space of perfection where nothing is lacking, and nothing is in excess, there is human suffering. We cannot escape it. We can make it bearable, we can overlay it with fleeting periods of happiness, possessions, and a million distractions, but the suffering is always there in the background, hanging around like a dark cloud.

Life is beautiful, it is a gift. There is so much to be grateful for, and yet it is also painful and tragic. Just like in quantum physics, where it's possible for particles to be in two different states at the same time, we too seem to be in two simultaneous states of being. One is like peace and one is like war. One feels like heaven and the other more like hell. One is perfect clarity and order, the other is confusion and chaos.

The way is perfect. Existence, life and creation are perfectly balanced, nothing is lacking and nothing is in excess. This perfection exists in each of us – we can feel it at times in meditation or in fleeting moments of grace, but in our perception the opposite is also present.

How do we live with, reconcile or heal these two opposing states of being? This is something you may want to explore in your journal through writing or drawing. Some of the things that come to mind for me are faith, acceptance, compassion, love and purpose. We can have faith that there is a higher purpose and order to things. We can accept that life is a mystery beyond our understanding. We can develop compassion for all sentient beings in the knowing that we all suffer in some way or will suffer at various times in our life. We can simply love ourselves, humanity and creation, and find a purpose larger than ourselves, do some good, and hopefully leave the world a better place.

I hope you enjoy exploring, writing, drawing and colouring in your journal. Here, within these pages, your boundless, ingenious soul can find expression, space and the freedom to be. Just as it is. Write, draw, colour and create to your heart's content. Then, take that energy beyond these pages and live to your soul's delight.

About my work....

Art and writing are my therapy. There is no singular meaning in any of my works, and ultimately, within their layers of intent and significance, there may be no meaning at all.

When I work, I don't think about what I am doing. I don't pre-imagine or try to figure anything out. I let go of expectation, step into timelessness and enter a deep, soulful connection with the present moment. If my work moves you in some way, that is wonderful. Perhaps we have made a connection that will transcend space and time. Whether it is now or in a thousand years, it makes no difference. I hope something in my work resounds and awakens the beauty and infinite creativity within you.

Love and blessings,

Toni

An Affirmation:

Begin with the Intent in Mind

You may like to start your journaling journey by pronouncing the following out loud:

I own my desire to express all I feel — my hopes, my dreams, my frustrations, my confusion. I search for meaning and purpose. I want to find it. My words flow from my soul. I communicate clearly, honestly and compassionately. I breathe in and realise my connection to the beauty and wonder of life. I am journeying with this planet and all of creation.

My life is a divine expression of all my soul has chosen to experience.

Within these pages, I am safe to free my thoughts, feelings and impulses without judgment, analysis or censorship. I write daily for reflection, for solace and to find peace in the stillness between thoughts, outside of words.

I channel the love, light and creativity inside me. The universal mind and the heart of creation flow through me also. Endless love and unfettered creativity erupt onto these pages. Journaling is meditative. If ever I feel blocked or stuck, I will relax and remind myself no errors are possible. Everything I have to say and express is valid.

I am energetically connected to everyone and everything around me. My true nature transcends time and space. There is no separation between the past, present and future. I am now, I am always.

*I freely express my thoughts, feelings and impulses without judgment, analysis or censorship. I practice this daily without concern for the results. I think of myself as a channel for universal energy. I **feel it flow** through me. I treat this as I would a meditation practice. Any time I feel blocked or stuck I will know my analytical mind is trying to take over. I am surrounded by infinite love.*

I am a seed of creation.
Within me lies all knowledge,
wisdom and possibility.

Today, I allow light and space into my heart, thoughts and dreams.

Today, I ***plant*** *a seed of* ***loving kindness.***

*Think about how this moment, **here and now,** contains all eternity. Past, present and future are one. **Life is a continuous flow.** Let your writing begin....*

Time is the movement of spirit — a record of my soul's journey.

Today, I ask my heart to speak. To perhaps reveal something kept hidden — a desire, a wish, a concern, a fear, or simply a message that I need to hear.

I live in accord with what feels right and true to me at this moment. However, I do remember that my opinion, my truth and my vision are not shared by everyone. Everyone looks at truth through their own lens. When there are a billion ways to experience life, perhaps there is no such thing as truth at all.

When you talk about anything in a balanced and open way for long enough, you are bound to contradict yourself. This is because everything is multidimensional. We change position to see the fuller picture. ***Creation itself is changing in every moment.*** *In a way, contradiction mirrors this. Life is beyond our understanding. When you talk about anything in a balanced and open way for long enough, you are bound to find there are many dimensions to everything.*

We are physically distinct but energetically connected. Our thoughts and intentions can affect the whole as much as our actions do.

A forgotten memory lay buried in my heart ...
Memories, scattered feelings and windblown pages
like autumn leaves falling.

"I am the sky, I am the earth, I am the air, I am life."

— Quick, without thinking too much, write whatever this statement prompts you to.

"I am blessed."

—Don't just say it, write about all the blessings in your life.

"My unique purpose and presence contributes to making the world a better place."

—Say this out loud, then write about how you contribute to making the world a better place. It can be as simple as a smile or a kind gesture as every little thing helps.

Today, I connect with the sacred power and wisdom inside me.

My creativity awakens and arises from a deep well inside me.

Whatever I wish for, I have already received.

Peace

You shall not find me
while trying to make sense of this world

Nor at times when you are fearful

For it is difficult for my light to enter the world of thought

Stop. Come rest a while in the shadows with me
I shall wait for you by the garden gate

Where silence shall be our voice
And all that is unspoken shall be carried by the wind
to ignite a flame in your heart

Time, space, dreams
dimensions of your soul ...
they are dimensions of love from which new life is born

There is infinite space within every atom of you
And, there is infinite and eternal light in every atom

Forever you are blessed by an innate love
that can never be lost

And so it is that you cannot lose me
Nor I, lose you.

"I guide others to the path of love."

- Write about how you already do this.

Without hesitation or thought, write or draw about how you feel at this moment. If you can't give expression to how you feel, make up some words of your own. You could start by saying, "What I feel right now, I am not sure of the words for, but here's some that come close ..."

"Nothing is insurmountable."

– Is this true?

In essence,

all is love

and through love

all is healed.

My awareness drifts to a place of infinite peace.

Today, I replace fear with love, acceptance and trust.

"There is a higher purpose and order to everything."
– How do you feel about this statement?

Today, I advance *with an attitude of* gratitude.

*Today, I count my **blessings**, not my faults.*

I let go of fear — and discover a shining star.

"Life constantly changes, nothing stays the same for long."
—How do you feel about this statement?

At some point, every negative will transform into a positive. At some point, every positive will turn into a negative. At all points, there is negative and positive. Both exist simultaneously. We usually see one side at a time.

in the land of
my dreams, I
of you and you
like an angel from
like the earth beneath
my feet, like a
within a dream, a
within a flower, a
within a world. you
came to me and
my heart and
my life with
in the beginning the wind
into our hearts and the
wind did howl and our
were united by the love that
moved the wind and by the
force that created love
one day the wind slowed
right down and the sky
still and blue and the
seasons changed and the
leaves changed colour
my soul expanded and
I embraced the earth
and loved you

Every atom of me is filled with light and creativity.

The past and future are connected right here where life happens – in the present. ***Now is all that counts.*** *You cannot change the past, but your current thoughts, intentions and actions will steer your future.*

*Be aware of the **observer in you** that is forever present.*

When I don't overanalyse things, I become infinitely wiser.

In meditation, observe how ***one breath*** *melts into the next*
and how each moment melts into ***eternity****.*

Perhaps nothing is predestined? Maybe it's all up to me?

I tap into and unleash my unlimited creative power.

Yes! I tap into and release my

unlimited creative power.

Today, I trust my ***intuition****. There is light at the end of the tunnel and* ***my future*** *will not be the same as my past.*

I am blessed.

"In being true to myself I am also true to others."

– Write about how this is true in your life right now.

I become lighter and brighter as ***I break free*** *of the patterns that no longer serve me.* ***I welcome*** *this time of* ***profound*** *and* ***positive change.***

Feel the grass alive and moving. Feel the trees breathing. All is alight with love. Feel a deep peace Settle within you.
Toni Carmine Salerno 2000

"Outdated systems and structures are being replaced by a new vision for humanity."

— Write about how you feel about this statement.

Within me is a young child who would like more light, love and compassion in the world.

I live and reflect the change I wish to see in the world.

How would you like the world to be?

How would you like your life to be?

Which of these do you have more power over?

"I think of you and memories glow like precious jewels.
I think of you and tears fall like summer rain."
— Write about someone you love who is no longer here.

An ocean of creative energy ebbs and flows in my heart.

In meditation, I envision my aura and love embracing the entire planet. In prayer, I ask the Universe to send healing energy to Mother Earth and all sentient beings.

I have often done what I thought I should. Now, I do what I know is good.

Today, I think with my heart. I do and choose what feels better rather than what I think is better.

The unknown is an exciting place to be.

*Today, **I let go** of fear **and** I trust that **all is well** in my life.*

Toni Carmine Salerno

the spirit of love
the soul of compas-
listen. to the whisper of your heart.
what is it saying?
love.
knowledge, wisdom
truth, compassion, beauty

Better to try and ***risk a little*** *failure than to never try and risk so much more.*

I ask the right question
and receive the right answer.

I am an ocean of love.

The past is behind me, I bless it and let it go.

When negative feelings and thoughts surface, I ***love and embrace*** *them, then watch them float away on wings of light.*

There is no singular centre of the universe. The centre is in everyone, in everything, everywhere.

I look within and ***discover*** *all I need to know.*

I see things clearly, not through searching for good or bad.
Clarity needs a balanced and neutral perspective.

Sometimes, the 'why' is known only to the soul.

A leaf is falling
smiling at the clouds
in total freedom
and trust.
The divine nature
holds all in its embrace
In the heart of a bustling city
In the soul of a forest
A glowing ray shines through
A lonely seagull glides over the ocean
While the desert sings its soulful song
A whisper
a cry
a child is born
and someone sheds a tear of joy
while
somewhere else
someone else
cries tears of sadness
The world goes on turning
The divine nature is present in all things.

***Peace is** possible no matter what situation or state of mind I'm **in**.*

The present is a miraculous place.

In light ***there is*** *darkness &*
in darkness there is ***light****.*
One cannot be *without the other.*
One is no ***better*** *than the other.*

I accept, love and embrace every part of me,
just as I am *this moment.*

There is a visible and invisible reality,
both are equally real and unreal.

I look beyond the surface and discover soulful wonder.

All of ***creation exists within*** *every atom.*

Love *guides me towards wisdom*
and compassion
and illuminates my heart
and mind in this
and every ***moment.***

Today, I meditate on the eternal flame of love inside me and all living things.

I am blessed.
I am safe.
I am loved.

all you see is me
all you see is you
light always shines true
through the eternal light of love
forever aglow within each heart

"An obstacle can sometimes be an opening."

A beautiful creation is wanting to be born through me.

Love's flame is in my heart.

I am a channel of ***light*** *and* ***love****.*

My heart *reveals* ***my truth.***

Today, I allow my awareness to drift to the realm of spirit.

There is a multidimensional space inside me
beyond the limitations of this world.

All that I am, have ever been and ever will be, lives inside me.

The present is full of infinite possibility, creativity and wisdom.

EARTH SONG

of time and space
and all that is spaceless

of trees glowing
in my heart
and wild flowers

spreading through vast
green
yellow fields
and spaces

of seasons past
and those yet to come

of oceans
unfolding
memories

and the gentle breeze

that blows
softly
caressingly

surrounding
embracing
recollecting

gathering
fading
into yesterday's light

Of this all absorbing life
and dream

and death
and of coming
and going

and of all things eternal
like the soul

of atoms of energy
flowing through the vast
spaceless space of infinity

and the earth beneath my
feet
the stars in your eyes
and moss
and leaves of the forest

and love …

*To be **free**, to be **at peace**, to love and be **loved** …*
*this is **my destiny.***

The language of the soul *can only be understood by* ***the heart.***

*“**I am** a force of **nature**.”*

I create, for it is in creation that I exist in this world of dreams.
In the stillness, the unknown waits for me like a void wanting to be filled.
I embrace life. I step forward with courage and strength.

There is no individual truth. Every person, every living thing, every tree, every flower, and every grain of sand, shares one truth.

Who created the creator?

At the dawn of time, I was a point of light.
Now, I am a trillion stars.

Beyond this earthly reality, *I am a multidimensional force of infinite wisdom, power and love.*

Something awakens inside me and I am forever changed.

Love is known through living, tears, laughter, joy and pain.

When this beautiful planet no longer exists, the life and soul of Earth will ***live on.***

My physical appearance may change with time,
but ***my soul remains*** *ever youthful.*

It is me that unlocks the endless potential *inside me.*

In the beginning, she gave birth to heaven and earth,
but the earth was void and without form,
and there was darkness upon the water
until her spirit filled all with light.

"I am a channel for the soul of the earth.
I am a channel for the healing light of love."
— What message will you share to this page today?

The beauty *I see in the world exists* ***inside me.***

When my thoughts conflict with my heart, I let both sides speak. I listen without judgment. I seek to understand the opposing force inside me.

I may not have the power to change *the world, but I have* the power to change *myself.*

Behind every mask is love.

Love *does not need a reason. It is* ***the reason.***

When my
dream is a reality,
I shall remember
reality is a dream.

The one thing
we all have in in common
is that we are all different
but only slightly different
for we are all part of the same tapestry
this is why there are over seven billion truths in the world today
and every day new truths are born
because everyone of us is part of the truth
each holds their own piece of the truth
no one person holds all the truth
that is why we can never agree on anything
until we join together and agree that it's alright to disagree.

Today, my imagination shall drift beyond my mind's horizon.

On a moonlit night, a majestic oak tree looks at the stars and rejoices at this wonderful world.

The child inside me wants to play and explore.
Let us hold hands and begin our adventure.

I don't need to improve, I just need to believe.

Existence is forever changing inside and around us.
All shifts, transforms and melts into the ocean of time.
In essence, we are reborn, not every lifetime, but in every moment.

As far as my soul is concerned,

I am always on the right path.

The Universe is listening …

Only in darkness do I see the stars *above me.*

"I ask my heart for guidance."

– Write down what it says.

*My **imagination** is one of my greatest assets.*

Let us ***strive to be*** *as* ***wise*** *as the trees and as* ***joyous*** *as the flowers.*